Praise for *The World at Your Feet* a

'An inspiring book written by an inspiring young man. A call for young people to transform their lack of self-belief and release their potential.'
Bob Wigley, former Chairman, Merrill Lynch Europe, Middle East and Africa

'*The World at Your Feet* is an inspiration to all those who have an idea but lack the confidence to turn it into a reality. I have seen young people in schools across the UK gain insight, courage and drive from reading it. It is a call to action for all those enterprising people out there.'
Lily Lapenna, CEO MyBnk and winner of the Young Social Entrepreneur of the Year 2008

'*The World at Your Feet* is an innovative book for anyone thinking of getting into business – or simply achieving their dreams. As a young entrepreneur, Sabirul really understands what's needed to be successful, and *The World at Your Feet* spreads that message to young entrepreneurs everywhere.'
Karen Mangan, former Regional Manager, Young Enterprise East London

'*The World at Your Feet* is an inspiring insight into the ideas of a teenage entrepreneur. Sabirul Islam thinks, talks and breathes enterprise and his book is a great way to tap into his approaches to success.'
Catherine Ritman-Smith, Head of Education, Make Your Mark

'Every student that reads *The World at Your Feet* cannot help but be inspired by Sabirul's example. His message is simple — "Believe in yourself and you can achieve anything." It's a powerful and important message for students not just in Swanlea School, but in schools across the UK. Expectations and aspirations are rising and I cannot help thinking that Sabirul has had something to do with that.'

Simon Firth, Assistant Head Teacher, Swanlea Business and Enterprise College

'Sabirul Islam, a young man who has illustrated the value of enterprise within schools through his book, encompassing the ideal of a true entrepreneur, and who has succeeded without privileges, just hard work, perseverance and a hunger for success.'

Nicola Arnold, Business & Enterprise Co-ordinator, Slough & Eton College

The World at Your Feet

Three strikes to a successful entrepreneurial life

Sabirul Islam

Marshall Cavendish
Business

Copyright © 2009 Saburil Islam

First published in 2009 by

Marshall Cavendish Limited
Fifth Floor
32–38 Saffron Hill
London EC1N 8FH
United Kingdom
T: +44 (0)20 7421 8120
F: +44 (0)20 7421 8121
sales@marshallcavendish.co.uk
www.marshallcavendish.co.uk

Marshall Cavendish is a trademark of Times Publishing Limited

Other Marshall Cavendish offices:
Marshall Cavendish International (Asia) Private Limited, 1 New Industrial Road,
Singapore 536196 • Marshall Cavendish Corporation. 99 White Plains Road,
Tarrytown NY 10591-9001, USA • Marshall Cavendish International (Thailand)
Co Ltd. 253 Asoke, 12th Floor, Sukhumvit 21 Road, Klongtoey Nua, Wattana,
Bangkok 10110, Thailand • Marshall Cavendish (Malaysia) Sdn Bhd, Times
Subang, Lot 46, Subang Hi-Tech Industrial Park, Batu Tiga, 40000 Shah Alam,
Selangor Darul Ehsan, Malaysia

The right of Sabirul Islam to be identified as the author of this work has been
asserted by him in accordance with the Copyright, Designs and Patents Act 1988.

A CIP record for this book is available from the British Library

ISBN 978-0-462-09952-1

Designed and typeset by
www.stazikerjones.co.uk

Printed and bound in Great Britain by
CPI Bookmarque, Croydon CR0 4TD

I dedicate this book to my parents,
for giving me the strength and belief
to follow a passion in life

Contents

Foreword

Is it just me or is it that everywhere you turn at the moment you can find someone talking negatively about something? As I write this foreword the three Rs are dominating the headlines – redundancy, repossession and recession – and there are research studies out stating that we as a society are more fearful of life in general. If we were invaded by aliens tomorrow they would not ask to be taken to our leaders but more likely to be pointed in the direction of the nearest Samaritans' office. In order to be successful it is a prerequisite to see the opportunity in any difficulty and to turn fear into fortitude.

This is why it is a great pleasure to write the foreword for *The World at Your Feet*. Having met Sabirul a year ago I was taken by the bundle energy that was before me; a young man who was not short on confidence and would not take no for an answer! In my capacity as a Cabinet Office Social Enterprise Ambassador and Child Ambassador for London I get to meet a lot of young people who ask me how they can become successful and they could learn a lot from Sabirul and his journey which is detailed over the following pages.

My own journey has been one that has some similarities to Sabirul's in that I started out from humble beginnings and I, too, used the ordinariness of my upbringing as an incentive to aspire and achieve more. Growing up in east London I took a lot of my inspiration from my mother who taught me some of the fundamentals that have stayed with me to this day; there is no substitute for hard work, treat others with respect, have good manners and leave nothing to chance or excuses!

Back in 2005 I became the first winner of the BBC TV show *The Apprentice* and was fortunate enough to work for Sir Alan Sugar, one of Britain's greatest entrepreneurs, for two years. I learnt a tremendous about from Sir Alan and the team at Amstrad Plc including how to focus on and use the numbers of your business to control its direction and how the team you have is as important as the strength and passion of the leader. I also learnt that nothing happens by accident and more luck comes your way the harder you work. However, the most important thing I took away from my time with Sir Alan was inspiration. Working in such close proximity to someone who had been there and done that and who empowered me to start my own division within his company gave me the confidence and knowledge to start my own entrepreneurial journey.

I am now the CEO of an innovative charitable organization called Bright Ideas Trust. Bright Ideas Trust supports aspiring entrepreneurs who are from socially excluded groups or who are currently not in employment, education or training (NEET) and helps them take the sometimes difficult steps to start up their own businesses. By educating young people, those like Sabirul and others, we aim to empower tomorrow's entrepreneurs who normally may not get access to the information, networks or mentors that are crucial for success. We are showing young people that business is for everyone, regardless of their background, educational achievement or socio-economic classification. After just four months Bright Ideas Trust has started and invested in four businesses and has spread the entrepreneurial message to hundreds of others through our website, workshops and social networks. Sabirul's journey proves, with a lot of hard work coupled with focus, what can be achieved is beyond dreams. Unfortunately, not everyone can get the support of the people who have assisted Sabirul or me. That is why I hope Sabirul's book will act as an inspiration to young people out here who are thinking about what to do next.

After meeting Sabirul through one of Bright Ideas Trust's trustees (Iqbal Wahhab, the owner of Roast Restaurant in London) and hearing about Sabirul's vision for 'world domination', there was much I saw in him that I admired and his drive and determination led me to accept his offer to write this foreword. Sabirul is not one of the negativists who I talked about earlier and definitely does not subscribe to the three Rs. I hope that if we are visited by aliens they land in Tower Hamlets and meet Sabirul who supersedes the Rs with Ps – Passion, Perseverance and Positivity.

I hope you enjoy his book and you take the steps necessary for you to create the future you deserve!

Tim Campbell, CEO Bright Ideas Trust
Spring 2009

Sabirul Islam
– My Story

Life as an East Ender

I grew up in the London borough of Tower Hamlets just a ten-minute walk from the City and Canary Wharf. Despite the nearby wealth of the financial industries, there was a lot of inequality in the area in which I was raised. I think that close

family and friends give you membership of a group, but where I grew up I realized that who you were as an individual and the vision you saw within yourself could make you believe that you were a 'sole army'.

I was raised for the first five years in Shoreditch, and there isn't much to look back on and say 'Wow!' That's normal for most people, but I look back and think, wasn't I supposed to enjoy my childhood, the beauty of being a kid? Well, maybe I'm overexaggerating. I was an individual who was born soft-hearted and I was always close to my mother. Wherever she went I had to go too, and for my mother that was pretty annoying. When I was three, my mother left me alone with my grandfather while she went shopping to where she thought was Liverpool, but turned out to be Liverpool Street. I cried my heart and soul out because she wasn't there. Small incidents like this make me realize, in a society where young people often behave badly, how your upbringing is so important.

I look back and savour the early life and bond I had with my mother, even though I was a pain in her backside! Looking at individuals who grew up a without a close parent in the East End, I realize that I am privileged to be making the most of a poor society.

Living in my grandfather's overcrowded four-bedroom house, my father decided it was time to move out. I was around five years old at that time and moving from Shoreditch to the Docklands was something to look forward to, although I did not really know what the Docklands was. During the first year in my new house I had a car accident when going out to buy ice-cream from an ice-cream van. That shook me for a while and I got to learn that living in the Docklands wasn't easy. During my early days there, I also witnessed fight after fight and the occasional gunshot.

Growing up in such a way, school was very important for me. My mother told me that you are who you want to be, not what society tells you to be. So from that moment I put my heart into achieving success. Life in primary school was quite enjoyable – I made friends and learnt to achieve at an early age. I look back at this time and say to young people, yes not everyone has an easy ride in life, but why follow society and what it wants you to be? At a young age, especially in the East End, people want to create an image. Sometimes it is one that others look at, and then try to copy. But I see that as following what society wants you to be. Like other people. The message I got from growing up in the East End is: Create an image, but one that identifies who you are as an individual and what your mission is in life. Don't imitate others, because that is not who you are as an individual.

I believe that as an individual it's about making a statement in a society such as the East End which others look at and don't confront. That in itself is a challenge and an inspiration to a young person's life. But at a young age, I believe I tried to show confidence and belief to be able to break the barriers of being an ordinary youth in a London borough that sees crime and violence as a way forward and tried something unique and different to make myself stand out from those around me.

Family Struggle

Being raised in a so-called ordinary family is where I actually got my first inspiration from, the belief and strength to want to be different. My family, from an outsider's point of view, is not that special. OK, maybe that is somewhat true but I see my family as my greatest asset to success. When I am down they will always do one thing or another to try to inject belief and motivation. But my family does not have an easy ride in life. All families struggle. However, I believe the struggle has a purpose, it has meaning behind it.

My father is the one in the family who has always tried to keep the family going. Well he has, hasn't he? Otherwise you wouldn't be reading this! Anyway, he had the entrepreneurial mindset. He started his own garment factory manufacturing leather jackets for big companies all over Europe. He made money, lost money and most importantly, fed the family. But his early life wasn't like mine. Where I can say I had family support from day one, he cannot say that. He was forced into work at around the age of twelve because his family wasn't there to support him as they had gone back home to Bangladesh. They left him alone with his aunt, who wasn't easy going. Despite the pain of not seeing his mother at a young age, he wanted to at least to show to his parents that he could stand on his own two feet. His business portfolio grew in importance for around two to three years. Although he was only 15, he got bored with being just a garment manufacturer. He was constantly neglected by his family when he needed support for the ideas he had to make money. Back then in the early 1980s ideas were quick to come by and once turned to reality, it was relatively easy to make money. All that my father asked for was support from his family and the little cash injection required. He never got any of that help and I believe that is what drove him to be who he is today. Although he does not hold grudges, because he feels he wasn't wanted at a young age, he sometimes returns that lack of support to his once close family. To me family support is very important, and without it there are consequences.

I hear a lot of stories from my mother and father about how life was a struggle without family support and I try to make the most of who I have around me. My grandfather from my father's point of view always supported and favoured his eldest son, who is my father's elder brother. Whatever he did and wanted to do, my grandfather gave him all the help he needed. My grandfather was the type of person who was cautious in spending his money and only invested in what he felt was right, which mostly led to providing more support to his elder son than my father. I think that was very hard for my father to accept. However, I look up to my father, who did have a tough time in life, and I am honoured to have such support and togetherness from my family and I look to make the most of that.

My mother is someone whom I cannot live without. She had a beautiful life before marriage, which she will never forget. Life was somewhat different after she got married at the age of 15 and now she has a family of six children to look after and feed. In her early days of coming to London after getting married she had to cook and feed up to 15 people a day in a house that was truly overcrowded. With my father losing interest in work and no income coming into the family, my mother found it very difficult to feed me back in the days when I was an only child. My mother suffered a lot for me and not knowing any English back then it was difficult for her to get a job. At times my father wouldn't show my mother any sympathy and threw all his anger and frustration he faced with his parents onto my mother. With my parents not working they decided to claim government benefits and I view that as life as an East Ender. At times the government benefits weren't enough to keep the family and there was one time in our new home in the

Docklands when the bailiffs from the council visited because my parents were not able to pay the rent, which meant that we might have been evicted and made homeless. Life has been hard for my family and there have been very emotional moments; for instance, when family members left home, wanting to run away because they felt they were not shown enough support and love.

Being the eldest sibling I often had to take most responsibility for the mistakes committed by my brother and sisters and often when I got told off my mother would back me up, which put her in trouble. Yes, there were times when I didn't want to exist in this world but I feel that all of this was happening for a purpose and rewards would come.

For me, life has been tough because as well as the family's problems, I too had problems of my own. When I was 11, I was diagnosed with partial epilepsy. Although this did not mean that I had constant fits or was affected by strobe lighting, it did often catch me out here and there with the side effects from the medication I took. There was one time in 2001 when I had my first epileptic episode and that caught the whole family off guard – it was an experience that I would not want to have again. This once more provided me with a message about life: with only one life to live it's about making the most of what is around you to live a happy one. I believe it's easier to find problems than to solve them and that is what I feel the youth in today's world does. They have a lot of problems and face a lot of struggles in life. However, that is the easy part. What they find harder is solving that one problem that can help them bring light into their lives. That is what made me think twice about what I do and where I go to in life.

You're Fired!

The beauty of being young is that there is a journey ahead, and what I see as being important in my early days is the fact that I tried to build my own way in life. This holds the cards for future success. I often feel that it's difficult to say why many young people don't have that vision. One thing I believe is that it's not always about inspiration from the likes of Sir Richard Branson or Peter Jones, because families themselves can be great influences and inspiration to achieving success.

At the age of ten, I always wanted to do what my cousin, Kobirul Islam, did. Wherever he went, I wanted to go. He was a year older than me, so he was off to his secondary school, Swanlea Business and Enterprise College in Whitechapel in the London borough of Tower Hamlets. At that point, I was in Year 5 going into Year 6. He attended summer school at Swanlea and so I wanted to go, even though I wasn't going to secondary school that year. Swanlea was his local school, whereas it was miles away from my home, but that did not bother me. During the two weeks in summer school, he told me he achieved great things. However, I didn't. This was one of the things which influenced me to become the person that I am today. I was so desperate to go to secondary school and be a better student than my cousin, that I wanted to skip my final year in primary school. That did not go down well with my parents as they thought I was insane. Children are usually sad to leave primary school, and there was I, the complete opposite! However, the time came for me to choose my secondary school. My parents wanted me to go to my local one, but I didn't. Whatever my cousin did, I wanted to better what he had done. He told me that he had achieved a lot in his first year at Swanlea and so I wanted to go there too.

However, looking at how I grew up as an individual, I cannot say that it was a comfortable ride. There were bumps all the way. My first year of secondary school was the first proper challenge that I saw as life. I trusted my cousin when he told me about his success. It made me go to new levels at Swanlea, from being good to becoming a top student. I achieved many awards. Even though that made me popular in school, I did not use that as an advantage for the wrong reasons. Popularity is one thing which young people try to grab onto to exploit and often abuse.

Being younger than my cousin, I obviously had to go through what he had done, and every year he told me that he had been an outstanding student in his class. I always respected what he said and achieved, but it did often did make me jealous. However, I cannot say that I saw my cousin as competition because I saw him as an inspiration to setting high-level targets so that I could raise the bar slightly higher. That was the case for my first three years in Swanlea, until the moment he opened up his own company called The Royal Dragons with the Young Enterprise, where he was the managing director. His company designed and created calendars for the teachers at Swanlea. Nothing exceptional or unique but the fact that he was running his own business at the age of 15, that was pretty impressive. But his company wasn't doing well, so he employed me because he knew I was quite good with maths and finance. However, I wanted a challenge because I felt that there was more to life than just maths and finance. So I was instated as his production director. At that time I didn't know what that was, but it was a challenge. However, because I was with my cousin, who had a higher level of experience and had set me targets, working alongside him was very difficult. I was in his company for two weeks when I experienced my first real moment of failure – the time when my own cousin who had been my greatest inspiration to achieving success in Swanlea uttered the words 'You're fired!'

That experience was daunting at first. My own cousin, who I had the utmost respect for, uttered the two words an employee would never want to hear. This actually made me think! My father had started his own business, so had my uncle and my cousin, and I was working 'in' a business. It just wasn't right. Today, looking back at the moment I got fired, I see that as another step in the journey of my life. That was the moment when I saw myself having control over who I wanted to be and what I wanted to achieve. This was what I felt was the difference between people around me and myself. Failure for me is actually a form of motivation – a wake-up call! What my cousin said he achieved in the early years of secondary school, he actually lied about because he had the belief that I could become a great person who could achieve great things. He stands tall today and still has the belief that I can always improve and become more successful. He made me realize that success and inspiration doesn't have to come from the outside world, it's always there from those who are close to you. I always look back at the moment my cousin fired me and I thank him for it. His company that year made a net profit of £60. For me, back then this was like being a millionaire. Once again – he set a target.

Life Starts Here

The 12th July 2004. The day I turned 14. The day I turned over a new leaf. I no longer wanted to follow in the footsteps of others. I wanted to create my own legacy that one day someone else would look at, cherish and follow. Influenced by my cousin, this enabled me, at the age of 14, to bring into being Veyron Technology.

All young people around us have ideas, creativity and, most importantly, talent. But one thing they find difficult is to find a way to implement that idea, creativity or talent. I think what I found interesting through the dawn of Veyron Technology was the strength of the team I had around me – a group of six innovative and inspirational young 11 entrepreneurs with whom I had grown up during my life at Swanlea.

Through my belief in wanting to be different, it was important not to do the common thing in business: be a re-seller. Through using the important skills of business such as networking and communicating, during our first company meeting (where I was elected as the managing director and majority shareholder), we came up with one idea that attracted us all. Website designing! It meant that we were not going to make twenty pence profit selling a bar of chocolate. We were talking about much more. But at first, none of us knew how to design websites except for our IT director, Sumith Imtiaz. He was remarkable. Only in the UK for three years, he had mastered the IT sector inside out. It was very important to make the most of the skills and talent we had, and to share our experience in each sector of the business with each other. What Sumith did was take the rest of us to his house every day after school for two weeks to teach us the basics of how to design websites as none of us had the faintest of ideas on how the website industry worked!

During the early days of Veyron Technology, I found it difficult to keep the group together and focused on the business. It was difficult because everyone had ideas floating around and no one knew what the next step was. This required stability and also leadership. Being the managing director of the company, I had to gain strong leadership skills because without keeping the company stable, success would elude it. We overcame this by attending business seminars where we gained advice from professional businessmen on how to manage and keep the company stable. Each individual within the company needed to be committed to what they were doing. We learnt that challenging ourselves to believe that we can always improve on what we are doing brings a brighter tomorrow. That brought success into the company.

With Swanlea School specializing in business and enterprise, it was about making the most of the resources and contacts the school had. We first advertised our business in school by putting up posters and sending out flyers to teachers and students. The response was huge. Our first client was our IT teacher who wanted us to design a website for his wedding so that he would not have to send out invitations. At this point we did very little research on how much we should charge our clients, so we thought, let's put a price tag on it of £20. That, at that moment in time, felt expensive. Our IT teacher was delighted by the service, and the pricing. Of course he was – we got ripped off. Well, it was our own mistake and that was a learning point. We then followed up on the research of the website industry and found out that websites sold for prices in the range of £800 to £4,000. We were left bemused. But it did not mean that the company had to go bust. It actually left a story to tell in our business that was pretty funny.

Two weeks after that, we got down to real business. We went networking at places like ABN Amro, Morgan Stanley and Merrill Lynch and literally sold ourselves. This enabled us to get our first major, yes, major client. We sold our second website, designed for a corporate client, for over £2,000. Wow, at the time, what a success!

Throughout that year as a young entrepreneur, turning my vision into reality required self-belief and the strength of teamwork. The website idea at first was difficult because only one member of the company knew how to design them. So, he taught everyone in the company how to go about it. The essence of our teamwork was that we all had the ability to share our strengths and together we made a successful team. Each individual had the self-belief in their role as a director to pursue success through trying and believing that 'nothing is impossible'. That helped us gain motivation which then aided us to gain publicity to sell ourselves to the world.

Starting a business usually requires the injection of money. Something my father did not get. I tried to beat the market without money. I did not invest a single penny of my own money to grow the business. And it was possible. All the money made in the business was 100 per cent profit. That illustrates the scale of success I experienced in my first year of running a business both financially and as a young entrepreneur. As a team, we went through a rollercoaster ride which had a lot of ups and downs, but we learnt that showing intensity, integrity and intelligence will always bring success at anyone's fingertips.

Kid or Adult?

Life as an entrepreneur was both exciting and difficult. It did mean taking some time off from school in order to go to competitions and events, but it was well worth it. May 2006 was the month in which my GCSE exams started. At that moment in time I put my exams first over everything and anything as I felt that was what would take me forward in life. I had taken business studies, drama and a design technology subject, which related to what I did through Veyron Technology. After sitting my exams, which were pretty okay at the time, I got a call from my business and enterprise teacher, Simon Firth. He asked me whether I would like to go New York as I had achieved so much through enterprise in school. That caught me off guard for two reasons: one, it was nine in the morning and I had just woken up; two, it was totally out of the blue.

Merrill Lynch, who I have had contacts with ever since the age of 14, have told me that I am a unique individual who has been able to make an impact on my own life, whilst growing up in a deprived area. That is what caught their eye and so they offered me the chance to go to New York on a two-week programme called the Atlantic Fellowship. At first I wasn't sure whether I wanted to go because my friend had been selected but unfortunately he didn't pass the interview process. That meant that I was going to New York on my own with eight other people from around the UK, all of whom I did not know. On the day in late July we were meant to leave, I decided that I could not go on my own. The flight to New York was at 1 p.m. from Heathrow Airport. The moment I woke up that day at 9.30 a.m., I saw my mother right in front of me. I told her that I wasn't going to New York. She looked so angry and she told me that this was a once in a lifetime opportunity. I was acting like a child looking for excuses not to go. Then, at 10a.m. I got a call from my friend who had not had the chance to go with me. He told me that in life we are following a path. Sometimes that path is with others and sometimes it's on our own. That made me realize that it was my life and I had to be able to say yes, I can do things on my own. So, through the inspiration of my friend I quickly packed my suitcase and went off to Heathrow Airport.

In late July 2006, the UK was not experiencing a good summer. In New York, they were going through a heatwave. I loved it! I adore the heat. The first two days on the Atlantic Fellowship programme, we went camping in New Jersey. There were nine of us from the UK and ten enterprising individuals from the USA. That was the first time that I had been camping. There were flies, bugs and mosquitoes everywhere. We did certain tasks from climbing a 15-foot wall to the simple game of hide and seek. It was fun. Day three was more down to business. The Atlantic Fellowship taught me a lot, from a day running a business to learning new skills and techniques of entrepreneurship.

One thing which really made me cherish the moments in the USA was going to Dow Jones and the New York Stock Exchange. I was sitting beside professional traders in the exchange, who had spent years trading for a living. That was an incredible experience. I did something which none of the other young programme members did. I actually asked the guy I was sitting beside to teach me how to invest in the stock market. At least the basics. He took time off from his work and showed me step-by-step what to do. At first it was very confusing, but being good at maths paid dividends. There was a lot to learn and I will never forget those moments.

Having experienced the innovative Merrill Lynch exchange programme in New York, I was able to pass on my experience to the others in the company to make it stronger and more enterprising.

I was inspired by the former chairman of Merrill Lynch, Mr Stan O'Neal, who believes strongly in global philanthropy. He said: 'Take charge of your own life and your career. Be true to yourself, which is an old axiom, but I really believe in it. Find something you like and excel at, and define success by your own terms.' This drove me to believe in myself and to break the barriers which held me back in order to succeed.

Once again, that made me think. I had learnt a lot on the programme and now I had to put that knowledge into action. I searched online about investing money and there was a site which let me invest $100,000 of fantasy money using real live market data. What I did was invest all $100,000 on day one in a company I had never heard of – and what happened? I lost all $100,000 in less than two hours! That made me feel really foolish. But the beauty of fantasy trading was that you could always reset your account. And that's what I did. I spent three months trading in the fantasy market using the skills I learnt in New York, and to be honest, I got bored. I wanted to do the real thing. Early in 2007, I thought yes, now it's time. I opened up an account for trading and started investing in the stock market. I became a part-time trader. If my mother and my friend had not persuaded me to go to New York then I would not have learnt how to invest. That taught me a lesson. Taking opportunities at a young age opens bigger doors for the future.

After the Atlantic Fellowship programme, I went to college. The first thing I asked the principal was: 'What do you do for enterprise?' The answer I got back was 'Nothing'. That shook me, but it opened doors for a greater opportunity. What I did was introduce enterprise within the college where eventually there were 120 students involved in running their own businesses. They all entered competitions and enjoyed running their own businesses. That taught me a lesson. If I can bring enterprise within a college and inspire 120 students to have entrepreneurial experience, then what is stopping me from inspiring others outside of college to do the same. Once again more doors were open.

Breakthrough at 17

I was starting to be recognized in my area. Young people all over the East End started emailing, phoning and continuously asking me questions. I felt proud. Everyone saw me as a young entrepreneur and investor and they were impressed. So many of them were coming up to me and asking me how, from the age of 14, I became an entrepreneur and how I started investing. That made me feel like a celebrity. However, I was constantly asked the same question and I kept repeating myself, which became very annoying. But I felt that I had to take it positively. Once again that made me realize that there might be an opportunity to exploit this. They all wanted to start their own businesses and they were all looking for inspiration on how to do it. And looking back to the moment I had inspired 120 students to become entrepreneurs, what was stopping me from inspiring the entire UK?

On the 25th September 2007, it struck me that there was a way that youth can inspire youth. Something which other young people haven't done: write a book to inspire young people how to take an entrepreneurial route in life. Yes, you may have Sir Richard Branson, who talks about his journey as an entrepreneur, but I see him as someone who is far too superior in the business industry to inspire young people because they have a pessimistic view that they can never be as successful as him. That is what made me realize that I have enough experience to tell young people a story about the success entrepreneurship can bring to them.

It took me around three months to write and design my first edition of *The World at Your Feet*. For some, that may seem pretty quick to write a book. But the journey in getting the book published had a story of its own. I approached many different publishers to publish *The World at Your Feet* and was rejected by them all. They all gave similar reasons why they rejected it. First, it was because I was 17 and I thought OK, that's a suitable reason. Second, was that they didn't feel there was a market for the book. That left me mystified. Why, with all those young people wanting inspiration? The rejections did not make me turn my back on the quest of getting the book published.

On New Year's Day 2008, I self-published my book, which meant that I had to market it and, most importantly, sell it. This left a great burden on my shoulders, but I knew it was possible. Once *The World at Your Feet* was published, it opened the door straight away to public speaking. In late January, I was invited by the Specialist Schools and Academies Trust to speak to and inspire enterprise coordinators and head teachers from over 250 business and enterprise specialist schools. The market was there. Getting the book into as many schools as possible was my vision and that was a fantastic way to do it. Everything looked like it was falling into place.

From 1st January to the end of the academic year, I have to say I found the world at my feet. Having spoken at over 300 different secondary schools, academies and colleges across the UK, I sold over 40,000 copies of my self-published edition of *The World at Your Feet*. The book helped inspire young people that through following the 'three strikes to success' they would be able to start an entrepreneurial empire that might one day leave a legacy behind.

The success behind my journey as an entrepreneur, investor and author sent out a strong message, especially to the publishers who rejected my book. Now, I was approached by publishers. I couldn't stop laughing! This time the message I gave them was that if you had believed that my book would sell then I would have been happy for you to publish it. The fact that I've sold over 40,000 copies, and the success you see behind it, was through my belief and determination that I could make the book a success without the help of those publishers. So, this time, it was me who was rejecting them. That felt good. But there came a moment when I felt that I had reached the limits of what I could do as a self-publisher. Having continually networked online I came across a unique individual called Tina Bettison, who had experience in the publishing and book industry. Through her extraordinary number of contacts, I was put in touch with Marshall Cavendish. For me personally, Marshall Cavendish ticked all the boxes and their intention is to make *The World at Your Feet* a very successful book. This feels very satisfying.

On 11th March 2008, the National Enterprise Academy was launched at my secondary school, Swanlea Business and

Enterprise College. It was a joint initiative by the government and *Dragons' Den* investor Peter Jones. He was there with the Prime Minister Gordon Brown together with other ministers. I was a guest speaker alongside them and it was a day to remember. The academy has been launched to give the nation the 'I can' mentality to teach entrepreneurship and I could see an opportunity to be someone who could inspire and motivate the 16 to 19-year-old students.

Having started my entrepreneurial journey at the age of 14, I have since been inspired by all the dragons from *Dragons' Den*, especially Peter Jones. I see him as a great inspiration for any young person because what he has achieved through trying and never giving up illustrates the intensity and integrity which he has. As an entrepreneur, having self-belief and understanding that failure is a learning point could only mean a successful tomorrow. With this attitude Peter Jones has developed an important business empire. He is a great inspiration for a young entrepreneur to follow. That's why I think that if he could achieve success through believing that 'nothing is impossible' then so could I. Through that belief and inspiration *The World at Your Feet* has opened so many doors for me, from winning the Mosaic Entrepreneur of the Year 2007 and receiving the award from the Prince of Wales, to being a Make Your Mark ambassador promoting enterprise and a role model for today's youth.

One of the good things about being 17 was the fact that new

opportunities always came to my door because the service I offered, and who I was as an individual, were wanted by other people. That truly felt rewarding. In late April 2008, I was recognized by ICIC (Initiative for a Competitive Inner City), which is supported by Merrill Lynch, as one of the most successful young entrepreneurs from an ethnic background in the UK. I was taken to Boston, Massachusetts, to be given the 'Growing Up CEO Award' by Professor Michael E. Porter from Harvard University. I felt that my achievements wouldn't have been possible without the support from family, friends and the organizations that have been there giving me opportunities to do something with my life.

Although this was the second time I had travelled to America, it was more of a struggle for me personally in Boston than in New York. On the second day, having attended Harvard University in Cambridge, Massachusetts, the group of successful entrepreneurs I was with was leaving the university. The moment I stepped outside the university, I had an epileptic episode. I fell face down onto the ground, which was full of stones. I didn't feel anything but the impact caused a lot of damage to my face and my arm. I had to go to hospital and the pain I was in, after I realized the effects of the stroke, was quite agonizing. I missed all the events that following evening including a baseball match at Fenway Park. However, having made an award-winning trip to Boston, I just did not want to be seen or remembered as 'the guy who had a fit', so the following day I still gave my speech even though I had cuts and bruises all over my face. For me, that illustrated inner strength and the determination that I do not want to let my illness stop me from achieving my long-term ambitions.

For me 'The World at Your Feet' looks like it can be nurtured into a 'brand' that can develop and become a trademark for promoting enterprise and entrepreneurship within the UK. Looking at where I am today and what lies ahead, what I have achieved is just a taste of things to come.

More to Life

Considering life as a constant journey, it has always made me wonder what life has to offer for the future. Now, at the age of only 18, I look back and question why life has been a rollercoaster ride, from the moments where I did not want to exist on this planet, to those where I cherished the success I had experienced. I see that my life as an ordinary East Ender is about doing something extraordinary to make a statement. But what I constantly say to myself is, 'Hey, I'm still only 18.' There is a lot more to life than just being an entrepreneur, investor, author and public speaker. Yes, for some that is more than enough, but I see that there is a lot more to experience in life than just continuing on with the same old usual stuff. Don't get me wrong, it's not that you should give it up, you should continue with what you're doing, but remember there is more you can do. It's about having the 'I can' mentality and that is what I tend to follow.

The good thing about being 18 is the fact that I feel more in control over what I am doing. Although that's not to say that my parents don't keep their eye on me, however it does give me the freedom to explore the world around me. Although the self-published edition of *The World at Your Feet* was very successful, I did not stop there. I realized that not all young people liked reading, so there must be something else available that would get the message across to them that they did have the talent and abilities within themselves to become successful. That gave me the idea of developing a TV programme to follow the journey of budding young entrepreneurs who have been inspired through *The World at Your Feet* from both the deprived and privileged areas within the UK and see how that differentiates. It will give out a message to young people that you do not need to have all the money in the world to start your own business. Ideas can be successful through hard work and determination. The vision for the TV programme does not end there. The budding entrepreneurs will be able to share their ideas with other young people. Of course, I'll be involved, it will be my own show. But the beauty is that the ideas will change and develop to become stronger. Even though the TV show is still an idea, it only takes self-belief and motivation to turn ideas into reality and that is why I feel the programme would be strong and inspiring for today's youth.

But why should it end there? A lot of people have been coming up to me and asking me whether I have taken on too much at such a young age. However, I witnessed my parents struggling and succeeding at a young age, so I don't see age as a disadvantage and therefore I believe that you can never do too much in life. Through that belief I wondered how I could benefit those at home who have the urge to experience the entrepreneurial journey but don't have the courage or are scared. It gave me the idea of developing my own board game. It was difficult to come up with what the concept of the game should be about, but with

the help of six young talented individuals, I found one. There is a maximum of six players. Each player has their own business, but each business has a different value. This underlines the fact that not everyone has the same amount of money and resources. Each player gets to run their own business, experience the stock market, use other business services and take out loans and investments. It has it all – bringing the entrepreneurial business world to everyone's living room.

Having achieved all this at a young age, I say to everyone 'Was this a crime?' Young people have constantly been neglected, which really puts them off when it comes to making something special happen within their lives. But what I see is that a lot of young people often watch the likes of *Dragons' Den*. All the Dragons are famous entrepreneurs, but one who stands out for me is Duncan Bannatyne. Why? He started his own entrepreneurial journey in the leisure and fitness industry at the age of 30. I compare myself with Duncan and other young budding entrepreneurs. Where he started his journey at the age of 30, I started mine at the age of 14. There is a 16-year gap. But I don't see that as just a gap, I see that as an inspiration because Duncan Bannatyne is now worth 'hundreds of millions'. It tells me that whatever I achieve in that 16-year period, I could become an even more successful entrepreneur than him. So what is stopping other young people from starting their journey young and possibly being future Dragons?

My 18 years have been a sensational journey, through times that have been rough, emotional and upsetting to times where I felt that a huge burden has been lifted off my shoulders with the success that I have experienced. To top it all off, '*The World at Your Feet*' concept is now being developed into a successful brand with further ideas including *The World at Your Feet* cartoon series to inspire the very young to believe in ambition and *The World at Your Feet* magazine. My vision for the future always requires optimism and through both the 'I can' and 'nothing is impossible' mentality, I sure believe that I will be able to have the world at my feet.

Are You an Entrepreneur?

Are You an Entrepreneur?

The Million-Pound Recipe

What makes an entrepreneur? Brains? Talent? Or a very good idea? Today's world is full of people who have turned their vision into reality because they were able to take risks and put their ideas forward. What separates a millionaire from a normal person is that they had the courage to look ahead and visualize what they would become and what they would achieve in the future. It is often the case that an individual like yourself thinks and dreams big thoughts about their own private land which they can turn into heaven. Yes, but why are you only dreaming? Why not make it a reality? Who's stopping you? There are so many questions you could be asking yourself and answering in order to achieve your million-pound dream by putting your ideas into action. Go out there and become the million-pound entrepreneur that you want to and should be. It's only a matter of time before the world is at your feet.

The Problem

Looking at young people today, they have the talent and are pretty clever but they have no cutting edge. The question which comes from this problem is 'Why?' Is it your culture? Your age? Or is it because you are afraid that doing something different will make you stand out from the crowd? At first, it might be scary, being different from everyone else. But it should be a risk which you are willing to take. Every successful entrepreneur took risks to succeed. Yes, some failed to achieve their goals at an early age but that does not mean to say that they gave up. All businesspeople face challenges which are difficult and what they find is that failure is a step forward for a successful tomorrow.

Being able to question yourself on why you're not making the maximum use of your talent is an inspiration on its own. Think of the positives you gain from trying to put your talent and abilities into action. As an entrepreneur you are your own boss. Think about it, you are the one in charge because the money you make, you keep. As a young individual you should not be afraid to take risks and use the talent you have and the ideas that come from it. It's only a matter of time before everyone will want to be you. So, who's stopping you from achieving what you want?

The Deprivation

Challenge. Yes, you should challenge those around you who hold you back. Being born and raised in a deprived area shouldn't mean that you have no opportunity. The world gives you everything you want and need; it's just you who has to pounce on it to succeed. I come across people both young and old saying 'If only I did this', which shows that they are only able to question themselves and their authority but do not challenge themselves in order to achieve their ambitions. Many people where I live seem to exist on money which is earned through low incomes or benefits and I'm sure they question themselves on why they are not like the millionaires and billionaires of today. I'm sure you even ask yourself that same question.

Why is it that young people who have such great potential keep the talent locked inside without ever letting it blossom? One factor which holds back today's generation of potential entrepreneurs is their culture. Being a minority in an area with very little income and people living as if they had no hopes or dreams should make you realize that being unique and different could be a step forward to achieving your entrepreneurial goals.

Young people wanting to stand out are often held back because they feel that they are not strong enough because of who they are or where they are from. This is often a reason that stops them from becoming the business idol that young people will look up to in the future. Whoever you are, if you have a great idea: PUT IT INTO ACTION! As a young individual, not believing in yourself is the common cause that stops people from becoming actual entrepreneurs. If today's millionaires can do it, why can't you? If you have a great business idea, then take that step forward. It does not have to be a big idea because small steps forward help you achieve big things.

The Big Question

Going back to asking yourself if are you an entrepreneur, well, are you? Young people like yourself learn from inspiration, whether it's from business people, pop stars or any other celebrities. Many are self-made millionaires who took that step forward to achieve their potential at a very young age. Famous football players, for example, start when they are very young and then blossom with amazing talent to become world superstars. When they look back to when they were your age, they knew who the world was, but the world did not know them. This is you right now. What makes you say that the world will not know you in ten or twenty years time? OK, this may be a long time in the future, but slow, gradual development and risk-taking bring great success. Getting there isn't impossible. Turning that 'impossible' into 'possible' requires self-belief and having the motivation to challenge the world, showing them that you too are a unique person who can one day be an inspiration for others.

One thing which separates today's young people from today's millionaires is that the millionaires always believed in themselves and they followed the right path to entrepreneurial success. Self-belief does sometimes come at a cost which can put a dark cloud above anyone's head. But that does not mean you should give up. Remember, you are who you want to be. Asking yourself 'If only?' will make you feel more depressed when looking back to how you could have lived a greater life. The time to blossom is now, not next week or in a year's time.

You are young and have the ability to be creative and innovative to turn your entrepreneurial vision into reality.

Three Strikes
to Success

Strike One: The Intensity

Do you have the intensity to become an entrepreneur? Not everyone's ambition is to become a businessperson; some people like to follow other paths, maybe become a lawyer or a doctor. But that's their own personal route which they believe will bring success to them. However, millions of people across the globe want to become entrepreneurs but do not have the intensity to do so. In order to achieve entrepreneurial success, the intensity requires control. Being able to have control and balance over what you are trying to achieve shows you that you are different from those around you. Everyone has different ambitions and talents which need to be used. This is never easy to do by yourself. Having the determination and courage to get help from others illustrates that you have the first of three strikes to achieve your entrepreneurial dreams. The negative aspect of life that others whisper around you should not be taken into account as that is a form of distraction. Be strong, and don't be scared to look for help.

Strike Two: The Integrity

Do you have the integrity to become an entrepreneur? This is not easy. Why? Because being honest with yourself can sometimes be misleading. Asking yourself 'Can I achieve this?' and saying 'I can achieve this' are two different phrases. Believing that 'nothing is impossible' shows great character. But for an individual wanting to achieve something which is beyond their capabilities shows them that they have the charisma but are held back for certain reasons. For example, having an illness can be a great barrier to achieving your ambitions. If you try and fail this can illustrate future success, but it's important to be honest with yourself. Continually trying something which you know you cannot achieve but refusing to give up could hold you back.

In the long run, you will look back and feel that you should have done something which didn't hold you back for trying. Again, this brings the risk factor into entrepreneurial success. Being honest with yourself, by admitting you cannot achieve something, doesn't mean that you should give up straight away. Having the commitment to show integrity could one day bring the world at your feet.

Strike Three: The Intelligence

Are you an entrepreneur with intelligence? Believe it or not most of today's entrepreneurs did not achieve their GCSEs or their A levels. But that doesn't mean you shouldn't too. They became millionaires through their exceptional ideas, but good academic results will help you beat the competition out there in the real world. Gaining your GCSEs and A levels puts you a step ahead of most of today's entrepreneurs.

After that, it's basically about putting your knowledge into action. Challenging yourself to beat the competition helps you to raise the bar in order to achieve the third and final strike. Putting forward an idea you have may face competition. Doing something differently with that idea brings success. The intelligence you have and use appropriately separates you from those who keep it locked in a box. Be bold and use your assets to build your own entrepreneurial empire.

The Empire

You may be questioning why three strikes bring success and not failure. True, they can bring failure but in entrepreneurial terms the three strikes bring nothing but success. The three strikes give an individual the assets to create a successful business. You look at today's entrepreneurs like Sir Richard Branson, the founder of the Virgin empire, and Sir Alan Sugar, the founder of Amstrad. They followed the three strikes to build empires that brought the world to their feet and they started gaining entrepreneurial business experience when they were very young. Now, here is the question: if they could do it, why can't you? If you're asked what brought success into your life, it doesn't always have to be that you have achieved greatness, it can often be how you approached success through learning from failure. This may sound weird but many entrepreneurs believe that it is a way that brings self-belief and dignity back into your life. Yes, failure is hard but learning from it brings not only success into your life but makes you feel more open to approach the world in a different and unique way. An entrepreneur's dream is often not to make the millions as quickly as possible, but to gain freedom through being able to put their skills and talent into action. The three strikes will enable you as an entrepreneur to bring out the best of your ability, making you believe that if the entrepreneurs of today's world can be successful then there is no reason that you cannot be as great or an even greater success.

What it Takes

Achieving the three strikes requires commitment not to give up. As the potential entrepreneur that you are, you have to push yourself to the maximum. Starting a business and then giving up illustrates failure. Be passionate about yourself, your idea could potentially help you start a new life. Be brave. As an entrepreneur you need to have control, to keep your ideas and targets balanced so they are not too difficult. Don't let your ideas run wild. Being able to control your ideas and imagination shows the intensity within your entrepreneurial capabilities. Finally, be able to face the competition. Being competitive will encourage you to be different and better than those you are up against. This will help get the best out of your entrepreneurial talent. It often takes time to construct a business that will operate to make healthy money, but trying to compare yourself with big-named entrepreneurs may be a downfall in your ambitions. Yes, you see them as inspiration but the distance between them and the ordinary person is far too great and this is what young people often look at and get put off by. That is why it is sometimes good to think about where you feel your talent can take you before pursuing overambitious plans! But that is not to say that you cannot be as successful as or even more so than Bill Gates.

Living in a Box

Think Big

You want your own crib? Mansion? Or even a castle? Why not? Are you saying that living in your boring old home, sharing your bedroom with family is a great joy? Think big – living in an imprisoned box knowing that you can achieve your dreams and aspirations is not walking towards success. Everybody dreams big, everybody wants their own land, mansion and castle, yet they just sit back like it's all going to come to them. Yes, it's hard to achieve but trying and failing is better than not trying at all.

Many people, whether they are young or old, love watching MTV. When you see those 'crib' shows, aren't you just stunned by the beauty of the homes of those people? It's almost impossible to stop keeping your mouth wide open. But at one point in their lives, when they were young, they were at a similar stage to you. They had their dreams and ambitions. You are young, and have your future ahead of you. Those famous people took separate routes to achieve their glory. Most of them put their inquisitive minds to the test. They took risks. Now look at them? Are you strong enough to stop living in a box? The world is not in the box you live in. Stretch. And set yourself free. Working hard now will bring rewards later.

The Big Equation

So, you've come out with an idea. Great! But it's no point keeping it to yourself. Think about it, you have just thought of a million-pound idea but you don't know how to take the next step forward. Many young entrepreneurs are so passionate about how they are going to make and spend their money that they forget to put the ideas into action. The journey of a thousand entrepreneurial miles starts with one step. Difficult you may think, but is it really? A small idea goes a long way. How? If you can put your idea into action by networking with the entrepreneurs in your business and with others at entrepreneurial events, the world will know who you are and they will want your service. It's about you putting yourself on the line. Sell yourself and your idea. Only then will that small idea bring you joy and success in your young entrepreneurial career.

SMALL IDEA x ACTION = MILLIONAIRE

Being young and inspirational, it's not hard to spread the word about your innovative ideas. Soon enough you'll look back at your two-bedroom house which you shared with your family and burst out laughing. Why? Because you were dedicated and motivated by inspirational people and followed the three strikes you turned that two-bedroom jungle into a mansion from heaven.

The Evolution

Don't let the world revolve around you. You revolve around the world. You are not a hamster in a cage, nor are you a human locked in a box. Peter Jones, who is one of the UK's successful entrepreneurs, said: 'It takes quite a while to come up with an innovative idea but a second to turn the world into your oyster.' You as a young entrepreneur will attain the world at your feet. You will be earning money to splash around and driving the cars you only managed to get sight of on *Top Gear*. Appealing?

I know. Your sofa might be soft and relaxing but forcing yourself off the comfort zone and putting your idea into action can change the 'I'll do it' to the 'Yes! I've done it'. That's what separates the millionaires of today from the people in your local area.

But I'm too young? And your point is? Being young is the advantage you should take forward to becoming an entrepreneur. Your mind is more creative and innovative. Your future is in your hands when you are young. Your creativity goes a long way because you can blossom with imagination from out of this world. Use it to your advantage. Anyone can become an entrepreneur. Really? Of course. All it takes is you being able to have the belief in your business idea and most, importantly, yourself. You are the greatest inspiration and motivator to yourself, so take that step forward.

Am I Really Bothered?

The Big Question

Am I really bothered? This is the question that faces every young person in today's world. It could potentially be a life-changing decision which a youngster has to make. Well, are you? Having great abilities without putting them into action is like saying that you bought a brand new flat screen TV but you don't want to ever watch it because you are not bothered. Be realistic. If you have something which is unique and can be used as an asset you should straight away be ready to exploit it. Your potential to become an entrepreneur is a start which puts you ahead of so many other young people. Many young people who see crime and violence as a way forward won't have a bright future. Your knowledge and abilities are greater than that. Every minute is precious, so spend it doing something you love. Any young person like yourself has ambitions to one day become rich and potentially live the perfect life. You not being bothered, that's crazy talk. Why? You live only one life, so to make the most of your opportunities requires being bothered. It requires being committed and putting your ideas into action.

Describe your everyday life to yourself. What do you do? Is it inspiring? Is it rewarding? And is it the life you want? Being able to question your motives for why you do certain things is encouraging. Most young people like yourself want to do something different, something fun. So, why don't you? It is all about risk-taking and being bothered. The sofa you sit on at home, for example. If the person who made the sofa wasn't bothered you would not have one to sit on. Being able to stand tall and always keeping your chin up puts you ahead of so many individuals who feel that crime is a way forward. The idea of becoming an entrepreneur is much more rewarding than those around you who influence you to do negative things. Be bold, your imagination and ideas are a way forward for entrepreneurial success.

The Type

'I had to make my own living and my own opportunity! But I made it! Don't sit down and wait for the opportunities to come. Get up and make them!'

Madam C. J. Walker
*(1867–1919, African-American businesswoman).**

Whether you want to become a social or commercial entrepreneur, want to make profits or to change the world, it means that you have to show that you really have ambitions. Sitting back, being lazy like other young people, is that what you really want? Or is it that you once dreamt that you will be driving your very own Lamborghini and living in a paradise home? These are two different things, but which one would you rather achieve? I thought so. And how do you achieve that? By taking risks and opening up your own business, whether it's on your own or as a team. Young entrepreneurial experience brings a stronger world for tomorrow, because your own ideas can change the world in which you live. Success has its arms wide open for any young person who wants to achieve great things.

*Taken from A'Lelia Perry Bundles, *Black Americans of Achievement: Madam C.J. Walker* (New York: Chelsea House Publications, 1992). Reproduced with kind permission.

You having a great idea but not being bothered doesn't mean to say the arms of success are closed. They are always open. It's just you who has to take the leap into them. How do I do it? Take risks. Your business idea can become very strong if you learn to communicate and seek help from all angles. Get off that sofa and let success give you that hug you want.

The Peer Pressure

Is it you? Or is it those around you? Who is stopping you from being that entrepreneur you can and should be? Being strong and saying it is yourself who stops you from being the entrepreneur you could be, illustrates the integrity you have within yourself. That's a strength which you should exploit and put to the test. Finding it hard, or believing that entrepreneurial success is not for you, doesn't mean to say that you should not give it a try. Starting up a business at a young age and running it for a certain time, just to gain entrepreneurial experience, isn't a crime. Young people often believe that they cannot run a business by themselves so they want to bring entrepreneurial success into their lives as part of a team. However, the common problem a young person finds is that they cannot put together a team. Should it be friends or family? This is a problem that distracts many young people from their own entrepreneurial success. Sometimes friends are not the answer. They may give you that little help you need here and there but at the end of the day, it's your life, your decisions and your success, but it's a step. Don't let those around you be a negative influence to your entrepreneurial goals. Avoid peer pressure.

The Deep End

Talent develops from trying and building on what you have already got as an asset. As an entrepreneur your aim is to achieve the greatest possible form of success. But is it easy? An entrepreneur always looks for the long-term success, so when you open your business, don't feel let down if you do not quickly become the millionaire you want to be, especially if the business has only been running for a short while. It is very important to take opportunities as they come but not throw yourself in the deep end straight away. Being an entrepreneur is like learning how to swim. You might at first be ambitious that you can achieve the greatest possible form of success for yourself but when it comes to putting your ideas into action, in this case getting in the swimming pool, your body starts to shake. Yes, it's difficult at first, but without trying you fail to live up to your ambitions. As an entrepreneur, always start at the shallow end then swim your way to the deep and more open end. Why? You will develop confidence to build your business empire, which could one day take on the business world. Like swimming, sometimes when it comes to running a business, many young people often don't get the hang of it. They keep on trying and trying yet they always fall at the last hurdle. Don't feel bogged down if you find yourself with this scenario.

However, as an entrepreneur it is an advantage to yourself that you have various innovative ideas which you can put forward to achieve your million-pound ambition. There are so many ways to succeed as an entrepreneur and you will eventually be able to dive into the deep end if you have mastered yesterday's shallow end.

It is often the case that a young person like yourself is pushed into the deep end because of what those around you have achieved. Their achievements are of such high standards that you fear that they will laugh at you starting from the shallow end of your entrepreneurial journey. No! You work and achieve success at your own pace. It's your life, so you have control over what you want to achieve and how you want to achieve it. Whether you are a minority in an area or an individual within the majority, it does not mean to say you have to be pushed into success, i.e. the deep end. It's about swimming your way to success by using different methods and, yes, you might have to swim very deep to build on your success but it's a step that opens the arms of glory which can help you turn your vision into reality.

Taking Risks

The Image

Bang! Straight away taking risks brings a negative image into anyone's mind. The negative image being the costs and the problems anyone could face. Why is it such a struggle, especially when a young person is to take a risk? Confidence. Self-belief. Two very important assets you must take forward into the business world. Every individual at some point in life will have to take risks. In fact, risks by individuals, young or old, are taken every day in all ways. Be brave. Be yourself. Believing that 'nothing is impossible' is a major risk to turn your vision into reality but it's a risk with a very little cost.

The Failure

What are the risks involved in becoming an entrepreneur? This is a very common question to which potential entrepreneurs don't have the answers, causing them to avoid opening and running their own business. The answer. Well, your idea not being a success. Before you put your ideas into action, images will continuously float around in your head, bringing future success into your mind, helping to put a smile on your face. However, any entrepreneurs, whether they are young or old, will always face problems, one being that their ideas do not sell or aren't good enough. Facing the reality challenge is difficult for many potential entrepreneurs in today's world. Both young and old entrepreneurs give up because their first idea wasn't successful. This does not suggest that you have no more ideas to put forward. Being an entrepreneur means taking risks. That is what's so special about these businessmen. The fact that they can visualize success but still fail doesn't stop them from trying again. That's the beauty of being an entrepreneur. The amount of times you can try is endless. Don't let your entrepreneurial life be short.

The Success

Risks. Failure? Not always. To be honest, entrepreneurial risk is a challenge you should be willing to take. It's not difficult and is highly rewarding. A small idea can make you a wealthy individual. Today's successful businesses, whether they are big like Microsoft or small like your local store, have had to take risks. No one knew whether the businesses would be able to succeed. Potential business forecasts and research help by showing possible markets and customers. Look at Microsoft today, the world's biggest company and it came from an individual's idea which he put into action. Who says that the idea you are putting forward and the risk you are taking cannot make you one of the richest entrepreneurs in the future? Bill Gates, the founder of Microsoft, took that risk and now has money which he uses to help people throughout the world. You are lucky because you have inspirations like Bill Gates to look up to. Putting everything you know into action is the step forward and remember age is nothing; it's about putting your intelligence where it should be which then rewards you for taking that risk.

The small often bring greater success than the big!

The Team

Still scared? Not convinced it's for you? Who says risks have to be taken alone. Businesses around the world today employ people of all ethnicity. This brings more ideas and innovation to the companies. When an idea is not successful, everyone is there to give support and help and take a step forward into giving it another go. Who says you can't do that? Teamwork brings success. Taking risks as a team brings success. Don't be put off when your idea doesn't match your team's. Put both into action. Take the risk. If you fail, you will share the pain but the unity and togetherness in teamwork also keeps an entrepreneur's chin up.

Never doubt that a small group of young, thoughtful, committed people can change the world

Learning from Failure

The Next Time

Failure is tough to take in as everyone knows. However, learning from failure gives you a brighter tomorrow. What an entrepreneur realizes from making a mistake is that the next time they try to achieve their goal they will do it in a way which doesn't cause them to make the same mistake. That guarantees a much more successful second attempt. New entrepreneurs don't usually give it a second try. Why? Because the first experience of failure was so stressful that a second would be too hard to take. The world revolves around trying. If no one tried anything, you wouldn't be reading this book right now. Despair? Never! Failure is a positive factor in entrepreneurial success. Having a great idea and putting it into action but then failing doesn't mean to say it's the end of the world. Entrepreneurs live off trying. Confidence and self-belief develop from trying. We don't know what the future holds, but we do know that putting your ideas into action and failing doesn't illustrate 'game over'. Entrepreneurial life doesn't survive on trying once. You must realize that learning from failure is a positive route which has a better outcome. You see anyone can make a difference, so why can't it be you?

The Marching Point

What is there to learn? How to fail again? No! Trying something and never failing is actually a negative experience because that does not challenge you to do better the next time. Failing the first time helps you set a target to beat when attempting to achieve your entrepreneurial success the next time. Many entrepreneurs of today experienced failure at one point in their business. That was a marching point for them. When a business fails usually a competitor wants to pounce. But when it's your company that faces the failure and you see your competitors advancing in your market, giving up gives your competitors glory straight away. You don't want that. Make them work hard to achieve their goals. To do this, you need to push yourself too. There is no limit to what you can achieve as an entrepreneur because what you learn from failure are new skills and attributes which you can use as an asset to beat the competition you face in your entrepreneurial market.

Entrepreneurship brings a marathon of success

The Belief in Everyone

It's not just entrepreneurs that learn from failure. Even the person you admire most, the person who you desperately want to be, took risks in something but failed. But they are still your inspiration, aren't they? Your inspiration failing to achieve something did not make you lose your admiration for them. That shows you have the courage to never give up hope when it comes to following your ambitions and dreams. Even you did not know that. At first failure might be hard to take but having belief in yourself and courage to continue trying illustrates your intensity in learning from mistakes. This is a great asset because it helps you to break barriers in order to believe that 'nothing is impossible'. As an entrepreneur you keep trying. At a young age you have the ability to get help from all sources through networking and that is a great step for future success. Handing over glory to your business competitors doesn't illustrate an entrepreneur's ambition. You want to be the best there is. You want to always achieve great things but to do this failure will come on the way. Don't be down when your idea doesn't succeed. Being young, you have the ability to put new and improved ideas forward to turn your entrepreneurial vision into reality.

Skills for the Future

The Inner Self

So you think you're an entrepreneur? Correct. Strong belief and determination, that's what an entrepreneur believes make a young person 'tough enough'. So, what is it that you gain apart from fame and fortune? You may be thinking that nothing else is relevant. Wrong. How you develop your inner self is what helps you grow your business into a global phenomenon. The world today grows around individuals who have the intensity to show that they are strong leaders. Entrepreneurs like Sir Richard Branson and Peter Jones have developed massive companies through being great inspirational leaders. Having strong networking abilities to communicate and interact with all walks of life illustrates talent which a business needs for dynamic growth. Having skills gained from entrepreneurial success puts your business with the best there is, because you know that you can strike back strongly if your competitors challenge. You have the intensity. You have the determination. That's what brings the fame and fortune.

Leadership

Leadership. Your entrepreneurial aspirations and talent will unveil a strong leadership capability within you, a skill which speaks for itself for future reference. So, are you a strong leader? Who says you're not? Anyone who has the intensity and integrity to pick up a team that's facing problems onto their own shoulders defines inner strength. It is an asset that says you are tough enough to be a leader. When you are young, leadership is like carrying an anchor. It's heavy but those who are capable of doing it are rewarded. Having good communication skills and being able to motivate others in your team illustrate your strength.

The future awaits. You are not the ordinary dispirited individual. You are the future. The future relies on you and your ideas being put into action. Being able to influence those around you as to why they should become future entrepreneurs illustrates your power as a leader. Leadership is not only an attribute which unveils your intensity as someone who everyone follows but it brings out the type of person and role model that you are and that everyone wants to become. Being a role model is an asset that all entrepreneurs have. It will enable you to strive for success. Young individuals will look up to you for advice and help on how they can turn their own vision into reality.

Leadership is not something which everyone is born with.

Often being a follower can be any young person's selling point. If you feel that you don't have the capabilities to be a leader then you are not alone. Why? Because you can look up to those who have succeeded through entrepreneurship and how they developed their leadership skills. Being a follower is often a stronger asset to have because you get to learn and develop your own routes and skills for the future. Learning to become a leader and role model through following brings greater success than for those who claim they are 'naturally' born leaders. You need to strive for excellence to attain your leadership and role model skills and only then will you enjoy the millions at your fingertips.

Teamwork

Teamwork? Oh, so you're a one-man army. Entrepreneurs have succeeded through individual talent and ideas being put into action. However, two heads are better than one. Why? Because ideas and workload are shared. Teamwork is always something to consider when you are striving to become a good leader. This means not only teaching your team members to work together. It also means becoming part of the team yourself. But what about the money? OK, the money may be a concern, the fact that it has to be shared. But in today's world, more money is made through teamwork than by an individual seeking to succeed. You want control? It's not always right to be the boss. You have decided to open up a business as a team. You make and sell your product as a team. That brings success. Occasionally, each team member will have control when you come across certain phases, because that individual has talent in that specific area of the business. But that does not mean they are the Julius Caesar of your business. You are young. It's a learning point. Being an entrepreneur at a young age opens the millionaire door much quicker than just wanting to work and earn at your local store. You are worth more than that. That's the strong essence of teamwork. The smile and the happiness, that's a skill. Why? Because success in teamwork will always bring the million-pound smile onto a great leader's face.

Money isn't Everything

Although money is very important to an entrepreneur, you'll realize that it isn't always the greatest of assets. And no, this is not crazy talk. Young entrepreneurs get to develop great charisma through leadership and teamwork that enables anyone to enjoy a happy life. Of course, money gives you almost anything you want. But the greatest entrepreneurs of today's world realize that money cannot buy you the friendship and bond that they developed on the rollercoaster ride they took with their friends and colleagues with whom they decided to run their business. It may seem weird to you at this moment in time. But when you retire before the age of 30 and are sitting in the grounds of your luxury mansion, you'll look back and wonder how life would have been if that team you worked with had not bonded and experienced the innovative entrepreneurial challenge. Questions are always hard for any entrepreneurs for tomorrow's world. Are you ready to put your ideas into action?

Turning Your Vision into Reality

The Market

As you're young, you may think turning your vision into reality is impossible. Wrong. Being young means being creative. Are you creative? Of course, you are! It's simple to walk the entrepreneurial walk. How? By knowing your market and the market knowing you. It's important that you know your market no matter how big or small your idea is. Who are your customers and what do your customers want? Young, you may be, but your intelligence is always there to challenge. When someone says to you, 'This is way beyond your capabilities' or 'You're too small to do this', prove them wrong. They are the negative experience for any potential entrepreneurs because when people like them say these things, the potential entrepreneurs take it without challenging them in order to prove them wrong. Standing up for yourself shows inner strength. That gives you the courage to prove the world wrong, letting them know that you are no person living on benefits. You are a person with purpose who wants to achieve their entrepreneurial dreams. So, go for it.

The market needs to know who you are. To put your idea into action requires innovation and excellence. Your marketing strategy is the heart of your vision's success. Knowing who to advertise to and delivering a unique advertisement that is different in the eyes of the world, separate you from your competition. Look at the challenges faced in *The Apprentice*. Each team has to put it's idea into action by advertising to the world. What brought failure to some of them was the lack of inspiration and creativity. Doing something different beats the market competition today. You are unique in your own way. Now put that uniqueness into action.

The Follow Through

Success is brought about by individual flair and also through teamwork. Setting up and running your own business whether it's by yourself or as a team at a young age will make you determined to achieve entrepreneurial success. Being able to experience entrepreneurial talent will encourage you to take risks and be very open-minded, something which entrepreneurs have achieved through dedication and inspiration. Turning your vision into reality at a young age will give you the confidence to follow through your ideas and what you feel is right when trying to achieve your million-pound ambition. Building the strongest team around you, which is not afraid to challenge, illustrates the intensity and integrity behind teamwork, which leads to entrepreneurial success.

Sell Yourself

As an entrepreneur, do you have the audacity to sell yourself? A little confused you may be, but that's the key to entrepreneurial success. How? Your idea may not always be one in a million. But you are. That's what you have to show to your customers, that buying from you brings greater joy to them than buying from any of your competitors. The market you are trading in must know who you are, more than anyone else. For example, the Dragons from the *Dragons' Den* invest in a company that stands out, where the entrepreneurs are able to sell themselves and their business on why they are the one-in-a-million. One very important way that enables entrepreneurs to be able to sell themselves is through public speaking. If you have the confidence to speak to an audience, whether it's big or small, then you are a shade closer to selling yourself. If the audiences buy what you say you will develop a unique reputation for yourself. Remember reputation is a strong factor to success. It may take years to build but it can get lost through the blink of an eye. That is why integrity(one of the three strikes) is very important.

What Next?

What next? A common, yet tough question. At a young age it is inspiring to set up your own business, especially with a charity that gives you the help you need through business advisers and offers competitions to sell your business to the world. Potential entrepreneurs often turn their vision into reality by setting up businesses with the help of organizations such as Young Enterprise, a charity that enables young people to put their talent into action and learn through innovation. Convinced? You should be. Being young and following your great inspirations puts you ahead of anyone else. Be dedicated and be focused. It may be a challenge but it's one that helps any young person turn over a new leaf and achieve their wildest dreams.

The Business

Don't do the 'Homer'

Lights, camera, action! This isn't a filming of a movie but the preparations which an entrepreneur has to go through to develop the best possible service there is. So, you've marketed your product. Your consumers know who you are. But that does not mean to say you sit back and wait for the money to roll in. No. As an entrepreneur you have to believe that success comes through trying new things to gain strong increase on the sales of your product. Your business evolves around you and your team. Set the team and yourself targets which are challenging but achievable. The business is not a toy where you can stop playing when you're bored. It's an entrepreneur's dream to be able to continue running their business to earn world domination, making as much money as possible. Don't be a Homer Simpson by snoozing off every time you face a challenge. You see, an entrepreneur's dream is to be the Mr Burns of the business. OK, he may not be loved but that does not mean to say that when you become rich like him, you won't be loved. Ideas come from imagination. Imagination comes through thinking. If you have the audacity to think, then why not think big to turn your business into an empire which the world cherishes.

Patience is a Virtue

So, you're not a Homer? Great! So who are you? Well, for sure you don't sit back eating doughnuts all day. You are a young achiever wanting to break the barriers to succeed. Your business will grow through opening the mouth of your team and feeding them with knowledge and ideas through which sales will increase and the business become profitable. Keep track of your finances. 'But I like spending my money.' The successes of today's businesses have come through the intensity to keep money and not spend it on irrelevant things.

OK, you may be young and when you have made your first couple of thousand you can get overexcited and feel that it's all you need. Wrong. When you have made money through your innovative ideas and then dump the business because you've made money which you've never seen in such quantities, it shows that you aren't strong enough to live your dreams. Yes, you've made a lot of money, but continuing on with your creative business would have helped you generate more money. Only then would you realize that continuing on with something which is a success has a much greater reward than giving it up because you couldn't control your excitement. Don't let money drive you crazy. That's an entrepreneur's rule. To you, thousands may sound like a lot but never giving up brings the millions a shade closer. Now, you ask yourself, 'not if' but 'when' your business is a success, which one would you rather have? The thousands or the millions. Exactly. Be patient. Only then will you be able to buy your million-pound luxury mansion and enjoy your relaxing jacuzzi. Mouth-watering isn't it?

The Off Day

Cold sales? It can happen. 'I don't understand.' When things don't go your way it doesn't mean to say that your business wasn't a good idea. That's the rollercoaster of a business. One day your sales could be a year's high. The next it could be a total slump. You don't have the power to control your consumers, but you have a strong say which can influence them. As a team, you should realize the importance of consumer demand. What your consumers want is what your consumers get. As a young person you must have a strong interest to develop your business further from the day it opens. Dreams don't just achieve themselves. Think about it. You place a light bulb above your head expecting it to light up. You'd be a total nutter to think that. But is it impossible? If it can happen in cartoon shows then why can't it happen in reality? Pretty weird but didn't that just make you think? So, to achieve your million-pound dream, your business must have the intensity to sell. Your product should be something which is demanded in today's world. 'But how do I know it's demanded?' Research. Yes, it can be boring, but that's life. To achieve great things and to become a millionaire requires a journey that will sometimes be fun but will sometimes be boring. Life isn't perfect. But as an entrepreneur you have the power to make it as close to perfect as possible.

The business only grows if you want it to grow. Slacking is a common mistake young people make. 'I'll do it tomorrow.' No. The way to succeed and bring glory into your young and enterprising life is to do things now. The business world has evolved through entrepreneurs doing things they believe are right straight away. You are young, remember that. You may know that it's a big risk you're taking, however it's one that can change the way you and those around you live, making it a more peaceful, fun and enjoyable life. You want that, don't you? Self-belief is all it takes. So, who's stopping you?

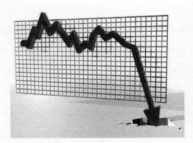

Sales slump – don't be put off

The World Laughs

What is it about young people today that makes them look for jobs at a certain age in chain stores or local shops? To make money? If young people think earning five pounds an hour is going to be a money-making career, the world will look round and laugh. Why? As a young person you should have the freedom to learn through big and inspirational things. That won't happen by working behind a counter all day or stacking shelves. You want and need to be up there working with the business side of the work. The directors. That's where the money is made. It's astonishing that young people look for the small things whilst having big dreams. Yes, you all want to be millionaires someday. But why is it that when asked: 'Can you do it?' young people say 'No.' Any entrepreneur will look around and be shocked. Why? Because young people like yourselves don't ever push themselves forward to their highest potential. Yes you've got your studies, yes you've got work at your local store, but that's not going to get you the money nor is it going to help you achieve your dreams. Success doesn't always come through studying. It can come from doing something different. Your business illustrates your role as a director and possible shareholder. That is already a greater asset on your CV than serving your manager's consumers at a local store. Are you an ordinary individual? Maybe. But it's up to you whether you want to work your socks off to earn the minimum wage or to work through your own ideas and ways to make the millions to turn that dream of yours into a reality. You're young, so use it to your advantage.

The Third World

You're living in a society that may be earning little but comparing the place you live in right now to the Third World countries, you earn tons more money than those who are suffering there. So, why not make the most of your opportunity? Those young people suffering will be thinking if only they lived in a society that is economically developed and has all the help available to potential entrepreneurs to turn them into the millionaires they would like to be. But you see, you have that chance to do it, and look around yourself. You know that everyone has the ability to turn their vision into reality yet young people like yourselves are the ones who seem to be suffering, earning very little money in an economically developed country.

You are not an individual living in the Third World. You have the opportunity to be the world's best. Now look at yourself. You are young and when you become a successful businessman you will have money which you can splash out on the Third World to help turn their visions into reality. When you take that step forward it's not just you who is benefiting, it's also those around you. Those who are actually suffering will benefit from your money-making business because you will have the courage to help them as they were your inspiration. If you had not looked at how they were living and realized how lucky you were, you might have not been inspired to take that step forward. Those young people want to be you. They want to have the opportunities you have. Yet you're putting them to waste. Why? Only you know. When you take that step forward to be the boss of your business, that world that once laughed at you will look round and cherish your success. If you are rich there are a lot of things you can do with your money to help those around you. Encourage them to take the route you have taken to bring success into their own lives. You are not just another human being. You are unique and have great abilities to help bring the world to your feet and also to the feet of those who need your aid.

You're Hired!

Change the World

Donald Trump? No. Sir Alan Sugar? No. You? Definitely. Put on your Armani suit and get ready to splash the cash. That's it, 'You're hired!' You have illustrated to yourself that your local shop's low- paid job was not your greatest aspiration. Correct? Your entrepreneurial talent now needs exploiting. Go out there and change the world. You are what you want to be. You will look back and you'll laugh at yourself. When you were sitting on your sofa and watching *Eastenders*, you felt that success would just come to you. You see the difference between you back then and you now is that you want to be different and that you have the 'I can' mentality which will help you exploit the three strikes throughout your successful journey.

You know you can achieve great things. You have the inner belief and strength to put your ideas into action, whether you want to be a commercial entrepreneur running a private enterprise or a social entrepreneur wanting to make a change to the world. You have dug deep and released something which you've always had but needed exploiting and that is talent. Go out there and show the world that you are no longer just an ordinary person. You are unique and extraordinary, with ideas that are worth the risk. And don't worry if you get coffee stains on your expensive suit because you will have the business and the money to splash out on your dreams, letting yourself run wild.

The World at Your Feet

So, are you an entrepreneur? That's a yes with a million-pound smile! Go out there and turn your vision into reality. If you need help, the world is your support. Like all the great entrepreneurs, you will become an inspiration yourself. Other young people will look up to you and say, 'If he could do it, why can't I?' And remember, you were once in that position too. Success comes to you when you want to bring it to your own arms. Who can say that you wont be one of those Dragons on *Dragons' Den*, risking money which once you only dreamt of having. That's the beauty that entrepreneurial success gives you. What success brings to an entrepreneur is more joy and glory. Only you can achieve your entrepreneurial success and find out what it feels like. Like they say, the world is your oyster and it's only you who can work to have the world at your feet.

Learning from failure gives you a brighter tomorrow

About the Author

Sabirul Islam is an 18-year-old entrepreneur who has grown up in an unprivileged area in London. At the age of 14, he founded a web design company which he ran for two years. He has experienced life as a part-time intra-day trader on the London Stock Exchange at 16, and lectures to and advises people of all ages from school, college and universities about what it takes to become a young entrepreneur. In 2008, Sabirul was the winner of both the Mosaic Entrepreneur of the Year Award and the Growing Up CEO Award. His new ventures under the award-winning brand 'The World at Your Feet' include a board game, cartoon series, membership scheme and an online TWAYFers Den, giving young people the opportunity to experience the life as an entrepreneur.

Top Ten Tips for Entrepreneurial Success

1. Vision – Think Big

It's often said that the young have far greater vision for what they will do to succeed in life! And from my own experience as a young entrepreneur, I couldn't agree more. It's a natural attribute every individual has, and it's the most powerful tool for entrepreneurial success. You want to achieve your million-pound dream and this requires you to think big, have high hopes and ambitions. That vision you have enables you to follow on with further ideas to make your business venture reach that level of success you want.

2. Three Strikes

Entrepreneurial excellence doesn't happen unless there is a philosophy to follow. Whether it is a philosophy of your own or someone else's, it's a matter of believing in that philosophy and illustrating the true values behind it. The 'Three Strikes' will give you the mentality to believe in your goals through showing the 'Intensity', the 'Integrity' and the 'Intelligence' as an entrepreneur to thrive on your journey. By following the 'Three Strikes' you will endeavour to find a route to excellence as an entrepreneur making ideas happen.

3. Belief

Believe in yourself! It is one of the simplest and most effective rules to follow as an entrepreneur yet many individuals out there struggle. You are who you want to be in life and not what society tells you to be. This is achieved through believing in what you can do and what you can achieve. Entrepreneurs take risks and because they have belief in who they are as an individual are not dragged down by the worry of how they are perceived by society. Belief is the key to everything.

4. The Three Cs

Whatever you do, you must show commitment. Without commitment you lose focus in your initial goal, taking you a step backwards rather than forward. Have control over what you are doing and what you want to achieve. Keep everything you do balanced, whether this includes your entrepreneurial journey or education. Remember it is not impossible to do both! Beat your competition. There is nothing more rewarding than doing better than the people you are competing against.

5. Feedback and Advice

Entrepreneurs never think that they are Mr or Mrs 'Perfect'. The importance of being an entrepreneur is to always raise the bar, and that happens through getting feedback and advice from people who see you as a unique individual who can always improve in what you are doing. Never think that what you have accomplished is to the best of your capability, there is always room for improvement. Get help, take feedback and always ask for advice. You will always learn something new every day.

6. Patience

Nothing happens straight away. But the beauty of being an entrepreneur is the journey you experience. Have patience in what you do and you will be rewarded. No entrepreneurs out there made their millions overnight. It's often the excitement and the adrenaline within yourself that will make you feel that you must do everything in one day. Do not rush to achieve your goals. Patience is a virtue!

7. Respect

Never get pride and arrogance mixed up. You may come to a stage where many people look up to you because of all your success. Be a role model, be an inspiration, treat everyone with respect and you will gain far greater recognition. There will be people who are always talking about you, mentioning your name, recommending your service. That is how businesses and entrepreneurs grow. Show respect and you'll be respected.

8. Network

Expand your network! Businesses grow through support and use of other people's knowledge and contacts. Go out there, talk about your business, your vision and there will be people who are happy to take you forward and up to a new level. Your business will grow and you will experience far greater success. 'Be the one who approaches rather than being the one who is approached.'

9. Charisma

Your success lies with the type of individual that you are. Having belief and confidence is one thing but people see you from all angles. Be someone who people think of as an individual who is easy to approach, has a great personality and is easy to talk to. It's often the simple things that make the biggest difference. Entrepreneurs are unique individuals who have their own sense of style, image and approach. But it's all down to who you are as an individual and having a good personality will make people approaching you 'instinctive'.

10. Word to Action

The most important step forward to achieving entrepreneurial success is to be able to turn your vision, your words into real action. Take that step forward into setting up your own business, achieving your goals and of course making your money. Nothing happens without taking action. Follow the ten tips and your entrepreneurial journey will give you '*The World at Your Feet*'.

Resources
and Contacts

Angels Den

Angels Den helps entrepreneurs connect with investors to secure funding through various routes in order to develop business ideas successfully.

www.angelsden.co.uk

Bright Ideas Trust

Bright Ideas Trust (BIT) is a registered charity which helps young people aged 16–30 to set up and run successful businesses. It targets its support at young people with potential but who are not achieving all they can, typically those who are currently not in education, employment or training. They support them with packages which include funding and hands-on advice and guidance from successful business people.

www.brightideastrust.com

Ecademy

An online networking website that helps you create business contacts that will enable you to pursue your long-term vision through the help and support of other networkers worldwide.

www.ecademy.com

Make Your Mark

Make Your Mark is the national campaign to unlock the UK's enterprise potential. It aims to create a culture that supports enterprising people to make economic and social impact. Make Your Mark works very closely with the media alongside corporate organizations to unlock enterprising talent.

www.makeyourmark.org.uk

Mybnk

A London-based educational social organization that provides young people with the skills to manage their money effectively and to make enterprising choices in their lives.

www.mybnk.org

National Enterprise Academy

Peter Jones teamed up with the government to launch a network of National Enterprise Academies across the UK. Their purpose is to identify the next generation of entrepreneurs. The first of the institutions will be opened in September 2009, and will be in the south-east of England. The initiative is aimed at Britain's teenagers aged 16–18, and will be available to those from all educational backgrounds.

www.neablog.org

Shell LiveWIRE

Shell LiveWIRE provides information, advice and practical support for 16–30-year-olds starting up their own business with an essential business kit to every caller tailored to their specific business idea.

They also provide one-to-one advice through a national network of local business advisers and young business mentors with an interactive web service, idea exchange and a social network.

www.shell-livewire.org

StepUP Foundation

StepUP Foundation is a global not-for-profit organisation that runs large mentor and speaker-based events that inspire thousands of teenagers at a time about entrepreneurship and life. StepUP's programmes are currently changing lives in the UK, Australia and New Zealand.

www.stepupfoundation.com

Unleashing Ideas

For one week each year, millions of young people around the world join a growing movement of entrepreneurs to generate new ideas and to seek better ways of doing things. Dozens of countries come together to host Global Entrepreneurship Week, an initiative to inspire young people to embrace innovation, imagination and creativity. To think big. To turn their ideas into reality. To make their mark.

www.unleashingideas.org

Windsor Fellowship

The Windsor Fellowship (WF) is a unique organization that runs personal development and training programmes targeting talented Black and Asian students in the UK. Their ultimate objective is to ensure that the brightest and best can become leaders irrespective of colour or creed. They do this by facilitating excellence in education, employment and citizenship.

www.windsor-fellowship.org

The World at Your Feet

The World at Your Feet website gives you more than just inspiration, it enables you to experience the success that comes out of an entrepreneurial journey and the beauty that arises from

being a young entrepreneur. The website has contacts, networks and resources for you to explore and use for your benefit that will enable you to bring the world at your feet.

www.theworldatyourfeet.com

Young Enterprise

With more than 40 years' experience, Young Enterprise is the UK's leading business and enterprise education charity. Its vision is that all young people will have the opportunity to gain personal experience of how business works, understand the role it plays in providing employment and creating prosperity, and be inspired to improve their own prospects and the competitiveness of the UK.

www.young-enterprise.org.uk